BUSINESS LESSONS LEARNED ALONG THE WAY

BUSINESS LESSONS LEARNED ALONG THE WAY

CHAPTER 26 - DOGS RULE!

PAT PERRY

PATSFITNESS, LLC
Mentor

Contents

About the Cover ix

Aknowledgemts x

Dedication xi

Preface 1

1. The Secret to Our Success 3

2. The Good Old Days 8

3. Making it Personal at Work 12

4. What Employees Remember 16

5. Get 'the Finger' 20

6. The Risks with Not Taking Risks 22

7. Why We Work 26

8. What Real Leaders Do and Say 29

9. Lead with Your Heart - Not Your Head 33

10.	Why Service Sells	35
11.	Define Success Personally and Professionally	39
12.	Women Need Opportunities to Lead	41
13.	KBL	43
14.	Put Yourself Last	45
15.	Be Genuinely Happy for Others' Success	47
16.	Never Negotiate Salary	49
17.	The Five-day Workweek is Dumb	51
18.	Dress for Success (it's not what you think)	53
19.	Wish I Had Some Answers	55
20.	We Need Another National Signing Day	59
21.	Few Benefit from a Merger or Acquisition	61
22.	All Standard Bereavement Policies Should Die	63
23.	Success is Boring	65
24.	Simple Ideas for a Happier Work life	67
25.	Over the Rainbow	71
26.	Dogs Rule!	73

27.	NoGoalz	76
28.	Size Does Matter	78
29.	No Regrets	80
30.	How to Market Your Company	82
31.	Social Media is Not Social...it's Just Media	86
32.	Ripples Cause Waves	88
33.	Imitation is Not Innovation	92
34.	Who Are You Working With?	94
35.	Meeting Expectations	97
36.	Always Have a Clear Head	102
37.	Work Does Not Matter That Much	105
38.	When You Know it's Time to Leave	107
39.	What We Forget	111
40.	Sweet Freedom	113
41.	Creating a Great Workplace	115
42.	The Last Leadership Act	121
43.	Miscellaneous Thoughts	123
44.	What I Will Miss Most	126
45.	What's Next?	128

About the Cover

I had some fun posing with our dog Peyton. She is a wonderful companion and fits every characteristic described in Chapter 26. We can learn so much from observing dogs' behaviors. If only we could do a better job following their example.

A special shout out to Mathew Huested, Owner of Prelude Photography & Video who did a great job capturing Peyton's personality. Also thank you to Kerry Marinchick for the front and back cover design for this book and my first book *Re-Shape Re-Define Re-Imagine*.

Perhaps you think it's odd to have a dog on the front of a business book. But, that is exactly the point of the entire book – to think and act differently. The status quo is just not cutting it and changing it starts with each one of us. Whether it is personal, professional or organizational success it can only be achieved and sustained by parting ways with traditional thinking. Woof – Woof!

Aknowledgemts

Publishing a book is not easy. It takes time, commitment and a host of people who provide incredible assistance.

Thank you to Brittany Feda who was the lead Editor for this book, and the dozens of people who read the final draft and provided constructive feedback. Whether it was content, spacing, grammar or format this production is the result of fantastic support from many individuals who gave of their time freely to help.

A very special thank you to my bride Patty for reading hundreds of my columns over the years and my two books. She is my number one editor, cheerleader and supporter!

Dedication

Employers – I was fortunate to have four entirely different work experiences that made up my career. Small, medium and large companies that provided me direction and new foundations upon which to learn. To those who took a shot and hired me at these organizations (Lloyd Foight, Bill Hopkins, Scott DePerro and Armand Lauzon) thank you!

GREAT People along the way – It was never the work and always the people that got me to go to work each day. Though there were a few 'rotten apples', the majority of the people I met in my career were incredible – you know who you are.

Family – Patty, Jessie, Matt, and Peyton – thank you for ensuring that family always came before everything else. I love you and am lucky to have you. You are my life.

Preface

In a blink of an eye, I find myself nearly 40 years removed from graduation day at the University of Dayton. Though I had no idea what I wanted to do, I was eagerly ready to take on the world. Through a series of fortunate events, timing and hard work, I had extraordinary experiences at four different organizations that comprised my career. Many of those experiences were positive, and some were learning opportunities. Like most people, I learned a great deal over the years at these companies, through observation and making plenty of mistakes.

Throughout the years, I jotted down these items, representing a mix of work-life lessons and beliefs. Perhaps some may resonate with you. As with my first book *Re-Shape Re-Imagine Re-Define,* I intend to share some thoughts that might elicit new thinking and inspire conversations at the workplace or home – thoughts that might help you be more successful, personally and professionally.

You will find this book to be a quick read and one that you can refer to from time to time. The chapters are not related so that you can open to any chapter as each stands on its own. Enjoy!

THE SECRET TO OUR SUCCESS

───────

For nearly 20 years, I was fortunate to lead an organization that focused on fulfilling its mission of making a difference at work, in the community and with our clients. If you have been at our offices, you have seen this Mission Statement displayed on a large and colorful canvas in our reception area. It's a constant reminder to each of our staff of what needs to be accomplished daily.

In 1998, I was recruited to a company (ERC) that was near bankruptcy, had a negative net worth and seemingly on its last breath. Fortunately, through the support of our

Board and key talent acquisitions along the way, we were able to turn the company around. Including this year, we enjoyed 19 straight years of profitability and an incredibly strong balance sheet. Proudly, we never had to borrow a dime and remain debt free today.

We expanded our business nationally, created a state-wide health insurance program (ERChealth) that saved customers over $200 million (over 17 years), established a nationally acclaimed program to recognize great workplaces (NorthCoast 99) and significantly expanded our professional HR services to area companies.

Our achievements were a by-product of our intense and unrelenting focus on innovating, having the right people on board and prioritizing our employees and their families over work. Ironically, we never embraced traditional measures of business success. As an example, our success as a management team was never measured by sales goals, profitability, or cutting expenses. They were measured on enhancing our services to our clients, new service innovations, and most importantly their ability to attract and retain top performing talent.

Our critics would suggest, that by putting our employees first, we missed opportunities to make more money. They would be correct. Yet if we had chased the almighty dollar, our employees would have worked crazy hours, not seen their families as much, and missed out on perhaps a better quality of life. We took the position that we would judge our success, not on how fast the company grew but how well our employees grew personally and professionally. We abandoned the popular concept of work-life balance. Instead, we embraced work-life imbalance, prioritizing life outside of work over their jobs. We knew that time away from work could always be made up, but time away from family could not.

This all started in 1998 when we radically altered how people would work at ERC. Give them responsibility for managing their work, their performance and their schedules. Allow them the flexibility they needed to raise children, care for loved ones or make positive impacts in the community. To make this work we needed to abandon traditional workplace practices and policies. Complete trust in team members would also be essential to making the program successful.We focused on hiring and keeping only top performers.

Aside from all our efforts on non-traditional approaches to work, we believed there was one factor that was tough to measure but would be critical to our success: employee happiness at and outside of work. We knew we could have a tremendous impact on both if we set up the right work environment. Of course, the pursuit of happiness is up to each employee, but we did what we could do on our end to increase the probability that people could have a more fulfilling life. We believed we could have it all – a very successful business with top-performing employees that had the opportunity to have a great life outside of work.

Back in 1998, we had not seen this done before, so we

knew we were venturing into new territory. There was no blueprint to follow. Fortunately, our bet was right as our employees enjoyed a unique and non-traditional work life as our business flourished. Today, we have seen hundreds of organizations across the country adopt non-traditional and very progressive workplaces. They know that if they want a competitive edge for attracting, retaining and engaging great talent, focusing on happiness at work is critical. For some companies, this will dictate substantial cultural changes, but the payoff will be dramatic. And, it starts with you. So, if *you* are seeking happiness at work, consider some of the following;

Define success – Assess what is truly important to you and write down your definition of success. Measuring your progress in life without this definition is difficult.

Find a GREAT boss! – A huge part of the equation of being happy at work is working with and for someone who you respect and admire. Bad bosses are bad for you and everyone else.

Find a great workplace – Ensure that the company where you are employed lines up with your values, your life outside of work, and definition of success. Companies like the NorthCoast99 (northcoast99.org) winners are a great place to start.

Get fit – Commit to physical, mental, emotional, and financial fitness. Getting there can be life-changing and life-saving. Your productivity will soar, your waistline will shrink, and you will be happier!

Spend more time with family – This one can be one of the toughest to implement considering many traditionally run businesses and restrictive workplace policies and practices. If you are the boss, let's start with you. Time to do something radical– the first week of the year, tell everyone that you expect them to be home for dinner with their family (unless they are traveling) for the rest of the year. That means you too. No work on the weekends either. And, if you respond that this cannot be done, then perhaps you should look at your organization's structure and the individuals you have on staff.

Try this new habit – Consider a random act of kindness toward one or two of your co-workers or people who report to you. You will make a difference in their day and yours.

So, the experiment we started in 1998 worked. We proved that a business could prioritize family over the job and still be quite successful. As we look back, trading off some dollars for employee happiness at work and outside of work was a no-brainer. I guess the phrase "money can't buy happiness" is true.

Just ask any ERC employee.

2

THE GOOD OLD DAYS

At the beginning of a recent business meeting, outside of our company, many of the attendees placed their smartphones on top of the conference room table. One attendee set up his laptop and began typing away. As the meeting progressed, phones were buzzing (with attendees doing the occasional glance to see what notification they were receiving) and the one attendee continued to immerse himself in whatever was on his laptop screen. He seemed oblivious to his surroundings and that a business meeting was being attempted around him.

It was not my meeting, but I witnessed in amazement this irritating, disruptive, and unproductive approach to an in-person group conversation. It dawned on me how far we have regressed relative to quality conversations, attention spans and just plain manners.

Somehow over the past few years, it has become acceptable for attendees to ensure they don't miss a text or email during a meeting. There was a time when the content and presentation at meetings superseded texts, tweets, or emails.

In fact, it seems that just about everywhere, the use of mobile devices is reducing face-to-face conversations. And, if it's not the smartphone, messages sent from laptops, desktops, and other mobile devices are serving as the core of our daily business and personal communications.

The dependence on electronic communication is easy to understand because it is simple, fast, and convenient.In so many instances the actual content and context of the intended message get lost in cyberspace. Before the *digital age*, business was conducted very differently than it is today:

- Conversations were in-person or on the telephone.

- Attendees at presentations listened to the speakers rather than "multi-tasking" on their mobile devices.

- We read and digested information before making decisions rather than reacting to real-time news through mobile device notifications.

- We got to know individuals we did business with rather than learning about them through social media and network portals like *Linked In*.

- Attention spans were greater than three seconds, which allowed us to listen and be focused.

- Real relationships and friendships developed, rather than relying on social media networks for recognition and companionship.

- Thank-you notes were handwritten, mailed, and personalized.

- Sales presentations and pitches delivered in-person versus the *daily dozen* spam emails that produce impersonal, hard-sell sales pitches from people we have never met.

- People dared to have the tough conversations in-person rather than using the keyboard to deliver the message.

- We recognized that a good career was a long journey of success and failures. Instant gratification was not in our dictionary.

- The telephone was used to talk and listen to others. No games, emojis, texts, emails or videos. We survived just fine.

Conducting business prior to digital communication was certainly not perfect, but it was simpler. Today the machines are smarter than we are, and they are getting smarter every moment. There are those who suggest that there will be a tipping point sometime soon when the fragile balance between our ability to compete with machines will tilt in the machines' favor. We may already be at that point. And, it does not help that the next few up-and-coming generations have been raised with an *electronic pacifier* in their hands.

Technology and digital applications are wonderful when utilized to complement and support our day-to-day activities at and outside of work. If we allow the best of who we are as human beings to shine through, while utilizing technology, the combination could be impressive.

For workers and businesses to remain relevant in the future, we will need to rely on what is our greatest strength; all the characteristics that make us truly human. If we continue to set these aside and allow technology to be a cheap substitute for our interactions and communications with others, we will lose more jobs, businesses, and worst of all ourselves.

3

MAKING IT PERSONAL AT WORK

I once read an inquiry on *Linked In* from an HR Leader in California asking her LinkedIn connections their opinion on the following: "If you need to terminate an employee that lives in a different state from their boss, does the termination need to be in-person, requiring travel for the boss? Incidentally, the employee to be terminated has been with the company for ten years."

I had to re-read this *Linked In* post a few times as I could not believe an HR professional was asking this question. The answer is obvious and has nothing to do with an employee's time with a company. Employment separations should always be in person. Though this posting may be an isolated instance, it had me wondering if some organizations and HR leaders are beginning to lose sight of the critical importance of treating employees as their most important assets.

Technology impacts how HR interacts with employees and prospective employees. Less time spent on in-person interactions with a greater reliance on communications shifted to technology solutions. An example is recruitment technology that, in some cases, virtually eliminates initial conversations with prospective candidates. These pre-screening conversations once perceived as a critical part of the selection process. Some organizations rely on technology to screen out candidate resumes that do not match up with certain keywords, phrases, or exacting specifications. Sadly, this approach eliminates some qualified candidates simply because a machine is "reading" the resume rather than a person.

There is no doubt that time has become one of the most precious commodities in business, especially for HR. Government compliance, doing more with less, and pressures to continually improve processes have placed tremendous demands on the HR department today. In addition, the role has changed dramatically over the past several decades as HR has become one of the most important positions in any organization. It should not be surprising that in some organizations, in an effort to become more efficient and effective their ability to attract and retain top performing employees has eroded. Though unintended, these organizations may be treating their employees more like robots than human beings.

There was a time, not long ago, when interactions and communications with employees and prospective employees took on a more personal approach than perhaps what we are witnessing today. Here are a few ideas and approaches that you may want to consider revisiting if your organization has inadvertently neglected critical needs that individuals desire at their companies:

Assess your systems – ensure that your technology has not displaced the human touch that people still expect at work.

In-person interaction – there is no substitute in the workplace for in-person conversation regarding critical communication topics. Two-way, in-person conversation allows for a constructive dialogue that most of the time, when done well, leads to positive outcomes.

Texts and emails – use text and emails judiciously when communicating work-related information. These modes of communication have their place when there is little interpretation needed with the message. Remember, your written correspondence is permanent.

Policies – too many organizations still have policies that had their origin over 50 years ago. Outdated policies like probationary periods and traditional bereavement leave programs send the wrong message to employees. Ensure that your programs and workplace policies are aligned with the interests of top performers today, including liberal work-life balance initiatives, flexible schedules, and a family first culture.

Credibility – your leadership team, including HR, must have established credibility with employees. Keeping promises, managing with integrity, and leading by example provide a solid foundation in which effective communications can occur. Having the right people in place in management is critical. You should have individuals at the top who have great empathy for their teams and lead with their heart as well as their minds.

We have seen workplaces with cultures ranging from terrific to nightmares. There are striking similarities with great workplace cultures – employees are valued, respected, and supported. When that happens, organizations can retain their top people and become known as an employer of choice for prospective employees. There is a way to embrace technology and, at the same time, prioritize your employees as unique and important individuals. It's just a matter of remembering to keep the "human" in Human Resources.

4

WHAT EMPLOYEES
REMEMBER

———

Take a moment and reflect on the people you have met in your career who have left the most significant impact on your work life.

Once you have them in mind, think about why you identified these people. Was it something they said to you or did for you along the way?

When I talk with individuals who are retired, they are quick to share memories of the good bosses and the special moments of their career. What we concentrate so much on during active employment (i.e., sales, expenses, goals, and business operations) become distant and forgotten items when people take account at what really mattered during their years of employment.

Interestingly, the traditional measures of business success are seldom thought of as the important stuff. What matters to many employees is being treated with respect, having security, working in a safe and clean work environment, being paid fairly, being recognized for a job well done, work-life balance, having fun at work, having challenging work, and being able to make a difference. I am sure there are more items you can add to the list.

Every day our company comes across local organizations where the leaders are putting considerable pressure on employees to attain aggressive sales goals, do more with less, and do whatever it takes to achieve the monetary goals of the company. And though employees of these companies dutifully carry out these marching orders, the fatigue and stress related to the unrelenting push to achieve more, unfortunately, leads to negative short- and long-term consequences to the individual and company.

Eventually, good people leave companies when there is a misalignment between their values and those of the organization.

Fortunately, we also know tons of companies that are achieving spectacular business results while maintaining and enhancing a great workplace for their employees.

These impressive organizations have a number of similar characteristics that include the following:

It starts at the top – no doubt about it, company leaders set the tone and lead by example.

Talent management is number one – attracting and retaining top performing employees is the top priority of the organization. It is a corporate initiative and policy that is communicated and well-understood by everyone in the company.

Family first – companies that prioritize their employees' families over work are winning the hearts of top performers across our region.

Community-driven – regardless of generation, employees today expect that their employers will support community initiatives.

Lead versus manage – the old style of management is no longer appreciated or welcome in the workplace. Employees expect their company leadership to be respectful, support career development, set a great example and provide an environment where innovation, risk-taking, and creativity are genuinely encouraged.

Open book – employees appreciate understanding what is going on with the business, well beyond a published mission statement. They want to understand the financials and enjoy having an open-door policy with top management.

Well-structured total rewards – individuals expect to be paid fairly for their jobs and performance. In addition, employees appreciate a benefits and perquisites package that provides choice and an array of meaningful programs. This would include a well thought out wellness program that provides employees with avenues to support a healthy lifestyle.

Do the right thing – companies that are admired by their employees are ones that always do the right thing even if by doing so there are negative financial consequences. Ethical and honest leadership is a hallmark of these organizations.

Respect in the workplace – in these organizations, everyone in the company is treated equally and with respect.

Life is short, and careers are even shorter. In a blink of an eye, retirement arrives, and the hope is that we look back on careers that were meaningful, provided a decent living, and filled with great memories. Sure, there may have been challenging times, but when I talk with retirees, it seems to be the good times they most remember.

The lesson that many employers are learning these days is that if they work hard to help create great memories for their employees, those employees will work hard to support the organization's success. And, that is something that corporate leaders should never forget.

5

GET 'THE FINGER'

It's not the finger you think.

I was pointed at a lot when I was a kid, in school and during my career. Behind my back and in my face, there were people who figuratively and literally, pointed their index finger at me to let me know I was weird, crazy, irreverent, unconventional, non-traditional, different, belligerent, or rebellious. Their words and actions reinforced for me, that the status quo was boring, traditional, ridiculous, and needed radical change. When I did get 'the (index) finger', I knew I was on the right path.

Perhaps I did think a bit differently and translated that into actions that placed me in the non-conformist category with some of my peers and a few bosses along the way. Yet, I never cared what others thought and interpreted their unkind comments as a message that I should not 'rock-the-boat'. And to this day, there is nothing more fun, fascinating, and challenging than taking the 'boat' to uncharted waters.

Not sure if risk-taking is something people are born with or learned. I do know we need more of it in our society to catalyze innovation and ultimately positive change. It just takes some courage and a bit of resilience when the finger gets pointed your way.

6

THE RISKS WITH NOT TAKING RISKS

A few years ago, I was facilitating a leadership session for a local business group. During the discussion, I asked the audience for their definition of success at their respective organizations. When asked the question, the attendees grew silent. Finally, one of the attendees raised her hand and responded that success for her and others at her company was "not getting fired". Her response was followed by several of the other attendees' heads nodding in agreement. I was surprised by the response. We explored the concept further as a group and discovered that many of the attendees were in organizations where it was in their best interest to play it safe, not take risks, and just do their jobs. Apparently, maintaining the status quo was the perceived goal of achieving personal, professional, and organizational "success" for some of the attendees.

Ironically, when I facilitate leadership retreats with top executives, one of the themes that consistently surfaces, is that they are challenged with ways to encourage their existing teams to innovate and take risks. In fact, I have yet to meet a business owner or CEO who does not desire new ideas from their team that will support the organization's success. So why in some companies, is there a difference between how employees act and what top leadership expects?

If this disconnect is occurring in your company, consider some of the following:

Set the foundation – Ensure that your organization has a performance management and rewards program that supports risk-taking, challenging the status quo and sharing new ideas. The concepts should also be part of your organization's corporate values.

It starts at the top – The organizational leader needs to publicly share with employees that developing new and better ways of doing things at work is a performance expectation. And, that the intention is to continually challenge the status quo, even if it is working. There is always a better way. The organizational leader needs to ensure that every member of his or her management team is on board with supporting innovation.

Recognition – Ensure that your organization is recognizing innovation, new ideas, and risk-taking. This can be accomplished at employee and management meetings in addition to company newsletters and other internal communications. The more public, the better. And, whenever possible, the organizational leader should be the one recognizing the individual or groups responsible for taking risks. Recognition can take many forms and includes promotions, compensation adjustments, gifts, or public recognition.

Recruit and hire rebels – Not every employee is a risk-taker. For your business to succeed and grow you need a core population of employees who are biased towards shaking things up and directed towards continuous process improvement. Hopefully, you know who these individuals are in your company. With prospective employees, ensure you have appropriate selection tools to be used during the recruitment process designed to identify candidates that are risk-takers and that embrace change.

The business climate is dynamic, and for companies to succeed, change is a requirement and not an option. To move forward, you need to have the right people, in the right environment motivated by the right reward structure being led by the right leaders. Remember, if your staff goes through the motions (which preserves the status quo), your organization will go nowhere (which is really going backwards compared to the competition), which is an awful place to be. The highest risk your organization has today is not to take any risks at all.

7

WHY WE WORK

———————

Do you work to live, or live to work? It's a good question and one that I use in interviews. The answer to the question is always interesting but does not tell the whole story about work motivation. The topic of *why we work* is fascinating and has been studied for decades. Depending on who you ask, "why we work?" will most likely be answered differently depending upon individual circumstances.

If you work, you probably know that it is easy to get caught up in the day-to-day minutia and lose sight of the bigger picture. Now and then, it's good to take a step back from the routine and appreciate the good fortune of working. Beyond the paycheck, there are lots of reasons we work. Though the pay may be the focal point, the positive impact work has or should have on each of us, brings to light how important jobs are to people. Here are some other reasons you may want to reflect as to why we get up early, sometimes work late, and work our butts off day after day for 40 to 50 years:

Self-esteem – Often people will cite a sense of worth as to one of the core reasons as to why they work. Feeling like they did something remarkable, earning a paycheck, and contributing to their company and community often play important roles on employee satisfaction and self-esteem. Being recognized for their job performance also contributes to self-worth and is an affirmation that they are doing the job expected. If any of these are lacking in a job, it may negatively impact their view of work, company, and their job.

Security – A fair and equitable compensation and benefits program should be expected by every employee in every company commensurate with the responsibilities and duties of the job. Pay and benefits provide a sense of personal security. Beyond addressing basic needs, pay, and benefits hopefully provide opportunities for wealth creation, for short and long terms wants and needs.

Friendship and human contact – Sometimes overlooked as a critical component of why we work is the basic human need for socialization. Good work environments provide avenues and opportunities for people to interact and develop solid business relationships and in some cases, friendships.

Making a difference – We survey thousands of employees each year at ERC, locally and nationally. Consistently, employees share that having a purpose in their job is an essential part of work. They tell us that they want to feel that they are contributing and making a positive impact on their businesses.

Intellectual stimulation – Work provides a terrific opportunity to be challenged. I do believe that all of us are inherently problem solvers and innovators. We just need the right work environment where we can realize our potential. Challenging work is also cited by our survey participants as one of the top three reasons for job satisfaction.

Being part of something – Ever since we were kids we wanted to belong to something. It might have been a sports team, a club or a scout troop. Regardless of the activity, as human beings, we have a need to be part of groups where there are shared values and interests. Work provides this opportunity of belonging for many people.

Hopefully, you are in a job that you like and in a workplace that has a terrific environment for all employees. If you are, then you probably appreciate your job, boss, and company. Work is a big part of our days, and as such, it is hopefully a great experience while earning some cash. If not, you may be just working to live.

8

WHAT REAL LEADERS DO AND SAY

There is a saying that "People don't leave jobs, they leave bad bosses." I am not sure who coined that phrase, but there is a lot of truth in that statement. How managers work with their direct reports has a huge impact on employee job satisfaction. A great leader can enhance employees' work-life experiences and be a major reason why people stay at a job. Terrific bosses combined with challenging work and competitive pay is a tough combination to beat.

As most people know, someone's title does not make

them a great boss or leader. In fact, the bad managers are those who utilize the power that comes along with their title to attempt to get things done. They are very authoritarian and unfortunately treat employees like little children instead of adults.

True business leadership occurs when power and title have little to no impact on employees performing at high levels. Employees who report to great leaders are motivated to consistently seek ways to meet and exceed what is expected of them on the job. For this magic to occur, leaders will tell you that the formula for success to engage and motivate employees is pretty simple. It's all in what they do and what they say.

What Leaders Do:

Lead by example – There is nothing more powerful for employees to see than their manager working hard, smart, and exuding professionalism.

Know, believe, and love – Managers cannot lead unless they know, believe, and love what they are doing. Employees see right through a manager who is going through the motions at work.

Care – Great leaders genuinely care about their employees and their families.

Coach – Leaders hire top performers, then let them do their job and stay out of their way. When needed these managers are there to coach, teach, and support employees to help them succeed at their jobs.

What Leaders Say:

Thank you – When put together, these two words may be the most powerful statement and recognition that a leader can make to employees for a job well done.

I was wrong – Leaders who admit mistakes earn the respect of their employees and peers. The boss does not know everything and is not always right. The manager, who acknowledges this, shows that he or she is human.

How are you doing? – A genuine interest expressed by the boss in their employees' well-being and job satisfaction is appreciated and noticed. And, this should not be confused with the casual "how are you doing" as you pass employees in the hallway at work. Leaders also ask about employees' families, which is another reflection that the boss cares.

What can I do to help you be more successful? – This is a great question asked by leaders of their direct reports. Great conversation typically occurs from this question and is often enlightening as to how to improve work conditions.

Great leaders naturally inspire employees. They also help make work more enjoyable, challenging, and engaging for their staff. Their impact on morale and the overall work environment cannot be overstated. And, as organizations are always on the lookout for qualified employees, remember that top performers love to work for individuals who lead rather than manage.

9

LEAD WITH YOUR HEART - NOT YOUR HEAD

We have made managing and leading people way too complicated. Ask ten consultants about how to lead a workforce,and they will provide you with ten entirely different answers. There always seems to be a new theory, approach, or concept that surfaces in business books, conferences, or with keynote presenters and facilitators. I have witnessed and been part of management retreats where the walls get filled with flip chart paper exhibiting diagrams, ideas, and brainstorming of how to develop, design, and implement organizational structures needed to support positive and productive work cultures. Sometimes all these ideas look great on paper but become seemingly impossible to make a reality.

I once attended a session at a regional conference facilitated by a well-known academic organizational guru. There were about 600 attendees present hanging on every word he spoke. I sat there in wonderment as to how anyone was taking this guy seriously. His theories were so complicated and sophisticated that answering the question of "What is the meaning of life?" seemed easy in comparison. At times I did not know whether to laugh or cry during his dialogue. Apparently,this professor had never spent one-minute working outside of his academic institution.

Long ago, I threw out all the theories relative to leadership and focused on listening to my heart. When you wipe away all the artificial stuff we have created in organizations over the past 100 years, you have a group of people who are interested in challenging work that has a purpose. When you get rid of all the garbage like ineffective and antiquated burdensome employment policies, layers upon layers of management and focus on your workforce as human beings, everything changes. Respect, empathy, and appreciation are all you need to lead people. Try it for six months. You will find a whole new world. One where you lead and at the same time create a culture where people will be inspired to completely rock at work.

IO

WHY SERVICE SELLS

———————

In four different jobs over 40 years, I never met a customer who was impressed or benefited from our sales record. Not one customer cared about our sales numbers unless it was somehow going to translate into better service. In working with clients over the years, I am convinced that focusing on service yields financial performance and organizational success far greater than when sales are the organizational focal point.

Unfortunately, gaudy sales numbers seem to excite some organizational leaders as they seek to grow their top line revenue at blistering rates. At these organizations there is pressure to accelerate growth, supporting a 'bigger is better' mentality.

Sophisticated clients are seldom impressed with the revenue size of an organization. These customers seek services and products that are high quality and delivered accordingly. From the employees' perspective, if they work at an organization that prioritizes sales over service, they are often left with more work, their same pay, and perhaps less job satisfaction as quality can suffer when sales growth is king. When sales rule, both customers and employees suffer.

So, if service has taken a back seat to sales in your organization, consider the following:

Service not sales separate you from the competition – Maybe it's just me, but it seems like just about every company touts excellent service. Unfortunately, not every one of them delivers on that promise. Marketing great service might attract some new sales, but if the customer receives less than advertised, the probability of ongoing or repeat business dwindles quickly. Conversely, your company will leap ahead of the competition every time you wow the customer.

Sales growth cannot sustain without service excellence – Your salespeople are going to be challenged in the market if your company has a less than stellar service record. Deliver consistently excellent customer service, and your salespeople will be genuinely excited about representing the company and passionate about its products and services.

Your sales force will expand – Deliver great service and your customers will serve as some of your best salespeople. In addition, your employees will be proud of how the company takes care of its customers, which will increase the probability that they will be great ambassadors of your business in the community.

Top performers will be knocking on your door – Having a nice workplace is only part of the equation to attract and retain talented people. Top performers want to work at organizations that stand behind their products and where quality service is the norm. Likewise, organizations need to have a significant population of top performers in their workforce to be able to exceed customer expectations.

Organizations that move from a sales-oriented model to a service model increase the probability that:

- Their turnover rate of top performers will be very low,

- Business retention rates will be extraordinarily high, and

- Customers will view the organization as a business partner rather than an average vendor.

Companies built on a customer service platform have a solid foundation upon which sustained managed growth, profitability, and success can exist. Let your competition chase new sales as you spend your time out-servicing everyone in your industry. It's analogous to the story of the rabbit racing the turtle. Let the"rabbits" in your industry hop all over the place as your company steadily follows the great customer service path. At the finish line, you know who wins the race.

II

DEFINE SUCCESS PERSONALLY AND PROFESSIONALLY

One of my favorite interview questions of candidates is *"Can you please provide me with your definition of success?"*

On a rare occasion, a candidate would provide a quick response. Most people when asked that question paused to reflect and develop an answer they thought I would appreciate. Interestingly I never cared much about the answer, but how they answered the question. If they had to think about the answer, it told me that it was a question they had not given much thought. And, I never hired a candidate that had to think about the answer because it told me that he or she could not articulate a core and critical element to their existence.

Defining personal and professional success is essential as the definition provides a life guide at and outside of work. And, depending upon what is going on with your life, the definition may change over time.

Once you have your success definition, you will have clarity and direction. It becomes the guidepost of your decision making and provides you a measuring stick relative to your life's progress.

12

WOMEN NEED OPPORTUNITIES TO LEAD

Wouldn't it be interesting to see what the workplace and our planet would be like if significantly more women held leadership positions in organizations and governments?

It might not be a bad idea at all to provide women significantly more opportunity to lead at every level. Perhaps we would see a reduction in greed, sexual harassment, corruption, wars, hunger, and poverty. I am guessing that Corporate America would also look very different. Issues like equal pay for equal worth, sexual harassment and 'glass ceilings' might actually diminish.

Men have held the majority of leadership positions since the beginning of time. How about women getting an equal say over the next 100 years? My guess is that things would be so much better with leadership comprised of a diverse group.

The fact that 'glass ceilings', sexual harassment and equal pay for equal worth issues still exist is incredulous. And, it is a sad commentary that in some organizations women still must play a man's game to be successful at work. We all know better and yet, sometime we just don't do better.

Having more balance, equality, inclusion, and respect at organizations and in government is the first step to an enlightened society. It is high time we got out of the dark ages and turned on the light.

13

KBL

If you know, believe, and love (KBL) what you are doing you are in the right place. Having all three is the perfect alignment at work and outside of work. And if achieved, the rare KBL alignment is tough to maintain as life brings new and different challenges every day.

It's how we react to changes in the KBL alignment that determines our fate. Those who adjust and work hard to re-align what they are doing in the face of adversity, are the ultimate winners. Those who allow even just one of the three critical elements of the KBL alignment to falter, find life less than it could be and suffer the consequence.

Determine what in your career and outside of work can

get you to knowing, believing, and loving what you do. That's the first step. After that, it is a matter of focusing your energies and activities on a daily KBL alignment. If you get close or achieve it, you will find that your life has new meaning and gain the peace we all seek.

14

PUT YOURSELF LAST

I believe there are two types of people in the world – Givers and Takers. Great organizational leaders are natural Givers and always put themselves last. They also seek ways to credit others for organizational success publicly and subtly deflect any credit directed their way. And make no mistake; employees quickly recognize the managers in an organization who are opportunistic versus those that are selfless and caring.

Employees respect and embrace leaders that put employees and their families first and the company second. And where this exists, you will find employees engaged with the organization, inspired by its leadership and committed to supporting the organization's success.

So, if you're looking to attract and retain top talent, be authentic, put your employees first and be happy with being the last in line. It is that simple.

15

BE GENUINELY HAPPY FOR OTHERS' SUCCESS

I've seen the 'Green Monster' in too many people throughout my career. Their jealousy of others' success is sad and misplaced. It is a divisive emotion that destroys relationships, productivity, employee engagement and happiness. Nothing constructive ever results from jealously of others.

Most people I have known through the years have earned the success they have achieved. And, the truly successful individuals are the ones that are most humble about what they have achieved or acquired as a result of their success.

I've always believed that when you can genuinely be happy for others relative to their successes, you are in a good place. Try to stay there in your life, as your energy will be focused more positively.

And, if success comes to someone else and you feel jealous, let it go or that 'Green Monster' will never let you go.

16

NEVER NEGOTIATE SALARY

If you get a job or promotional offer, never negotiate salary. Regardless of what you read or the advice you receive from others, salary negotiation is a great first step to take if you are looking to start the employment relationship off on the wrong foot. Quality employers make fair and attractive offers. And, if you don't believe that your offer is fair, simply continue your job search. Believe me, the couple of extra bucks you might successfully negotiate will hurt you in the long run.

Employers should always offer competitive and fair starting salaries and promotional increases. 'Low-balling' starting pay or promotional increases is just plain dumb.

It's a poor business practice and certainly says something about the integrity of your workplace and leadership.

Whether you are an employee or employer, the following rule often applies relative to salary and wage negotiation – "when you win, you lose".

17

THE FIVE-DAY WORKWEEK IS DUMB

When is the last time you heard someone say they were upset because of an upcoming three-day weekend due to a nationally observed holiday? Probably never.

Most people love their time away from work, even if they love their jobs and workplaces. And, some employers have attempted to increase opportunities for employees to spend more time outside of work by providing flextime and shorter work weeks (e.g., four days working ten hours). Even these forward thinking employers struggle at times with the challenge of balancing productivity with employee time off.

Incredibly, the five-day workweek had its origins back to the early 1900's. The five-day work week may have made some sense back then, but today it seems like a really bad idea. Virtually everything has changed relative to work and workers in the past 100+ years, but the majority of companies still stick to this archaic old habit.

Changing this structured approach to work is actually pretty easy when you focus on results versus time. Yet, too many corporate leaders equate performance with time worked. Perhaps they even feel cheated if a top performing employee, works less than a standard eight-hour day.

Life is short and spending the majority of it at work, does not make a lot of sense. Though some progressive organizations provide greater flexibility for their work teams, it may not be enough. The 'clock-watching' needs to stop. The next work generations will hopefully continue to put pressure on their workplaces to take a fresh look at how work can be performed without the baggage of a century old and unproductive eight-hour day, five days a week (Ugh).

Imagine a three-day workweek and four-day weekend. That would be a good start. I am not sure anyone would complain other than the 'dinosaur' bosses. And, we all know what happened to the dinosaurs.

18

DRESS FOR SUCCESS (IT'S NOT WHAT YOU THINK)

If there was such a contraption as a time machine, I would go back in time and ensure that the necktie was never invented. It reminds me of a noose and on tough workdays, it always seems to get tighter. Never really understood or agreed with the concept of dressing 'professional'. To me, it was never more than 'window dressing'. People may look nice on the outside, but it is always what is inside people that makes the difference.

I have met way too many people along the way that dressed 'professional' but were first class jerks. They dressed to impress until they opened their mouths. Give me a great person who comes to work in jeans and a T-shirt any day.

My most productive days at work were always 'casual Fridays' (in the old days) and any day that I wore an open collar shirt (or T-shirt and hoodie), jeans and sneakers. Comfort equals productivity in my book, and I did not even have to change into comfortable clothes when I arrived home from work! What a concept.

It looks like the up and coming generations have already made their workplace fashion statement and perhaps it is here to stay. Comfortable, casual and fun. Maybe I will be lucky enough to live long enough to see the demise of the necktie, a dying fashion accessory that is hanging on for dear life.

19

WISH I HAD SOME ANSWERS

I have been fortunate enough to have a career that has spanned nearly 40 years. Some people would expect that anyone with all that work experience would have answers to lots of questions about work and the workplace. Far from it. What I have learned is that I have many more questions about the workplace than I have answers.

Some of these questions are from my children, some co-workers and others from a variety of people of all ages and backgrounds. The questions would seem to have common sense answers and solutions, but with some exceptions they remain enigmas (at least to me). Here is a sampling of the tougher questions I have yet to figure out:

- Why do some companies keep doing traditional, annual formal performance reviews when most people hate the process and the forms?

- Why are there still organizations that do not provide equal pay for equal work?

- Why do so many people still go to a job they hate?

- Why don't we mandate psychological assessments and background checks for candidates seeking public office?

- Why are new employees put on Probationary Period at some organizations? Did they do something wrong?

- Why are professional athletes paid and praised more than so many other professions where lives are saved, diseases are cured and children are taught? And, why don't we ask for the autographs of these people instead of athletes?

- Why are office meetings always seemingly scheduled for one hour?

- Why do some organizations have candy and chips in their vending machines, but get upset about their rising health insurance costs?

- Why do some companies provide a list of people in their Bereavement Leave policies that their employees can mourn (with a maximum number of paid time off to mourn)?

- Why do they call it work/life balance if workers still spend more time at work than with their families?

- Why do some HR departments take so long to respond to candidates for open positions?

- Why do some HR departments never respond to candidates?

- Why are the spaces on some Employment Applications so tiny?

- Why do some interviewers still ask some candidates questions related to candidates' strengths and weaknesses?

- Why are there not more women represented on management teams and company Boards?

- Why are some CEOs of public companies paid so much money?

- Why do people feel it is OK to set their mobile device on a conference table during meetings?

- Why do some companies employ people they do not trust and/or are consistently poor performers?

- Why do we make such a big deal about a 10 year work anniversary but not an 11 year work anniversary?

- Why don't we always have 3 day weekends?

- Do 'Use It or Lose It' vacation policies still make any sense?

- Why do some companies still have a limited number of paid sick days for their employees? If the answer is that some people will abuse the policy if it was unlimited, then why are these companies still employing those people?

- Why isn't every organization committed to only hiring and keeping the very best talent they can find?

Perhaps you have a list of your own questions about work that just seem like common sense, relative to the answers. Too many companies still approach work and the employment of people in traditional and non-productive ways. The business world has certainly become more complex and challenging. Given that, perhaps it makes sense to ask these and other questions of yourself and your management team. The answers you receive will provide great insight relative to you and your team's road ahead.

20

WE NEED ANOTHER NATIONAL SIGNING DAY

National Signing Day, is the first official day high school senior athletes can sign National Letters of Intent with college programs. Much is made of local signings, and nationally, colleges boast about their recruiting class. There is no doubt that on our athletic playing fields, there are some incredible athletes that deserve and have worked hard to achieve and be rewarded with scholarship dollars at colleges and universities.

Likewise, how cool would it be if we also celebrated a National Signing Day for academic scholarships, or for seniors who chose to enlist in the armed forces to serve our country? Similar to local athletic programs there are great stories out of the classroom about area students' incredible academic achievements.

When I talk with local business owners, they tell me that their biggest challenge is finding and keeping talented individuals. For new entrants into the workforce, employers seek individuals who excelled academically, had a few internships, participated in leadership activities and were involved in the community. And, if candidates participated in athletics at some level, it demonstrates that the candidates' participated in team activities and competed – certainly a plus. Coupled with academic excellence, sports involvement reflects a well-rounded individual who was able to successfully manage their time.

Maybe one day we will have a National Signing Day for academic scholarships and schools will embrace an Academic Hall of Fame. Maybe one day, in addition to a Sports section, newspapers will have an Academic/ Professional section highlighting stories of academic and leadership achievements. Maybe one day children will idolize those who achieve academic and professional excellence, even seeking autographs from high achievers.

I know this all may seem far-fetched. But isn't it sad and scary that imagining, prioritizing and promoting academic achievement in this country, at least on the same level as athletic achievements, seems crazy?

21

FEW BENEFIT FROM A MERGER OR ACQUISITION

The press releases seem to be all the same that announce a merger or acquisition. The only difference is the names of the organizations. After the facts of the merger/acquisition are summarized there are the usual 'feel good' quotes from the respective leaders of the organizations involved in the transaction. Words like synergy, alignment, expansion, growth and of course the obligatory mention of how customers will benefit are utilized to provide the necessary 'window dressing' that the merger/acquisition is positive.

I cannot remember one merger or acquisition that really benefited anyone except a few people at the top, the lawyers, consultants and the respective Board members. Rank and file employees don't see more money, usually have more work to do and are stressed wondering if their job is about to be eliminated due to duplication resulting from the organizations getting together.

Bigger is not always better. Employees of larger companies have a greater challenge standing out, making an impact and getting through bureaucracy and politics often associated with larger organizations. That's not to say that all big companies are average. It's just that when a merger or acquisition occurs you often see great organizations become less of what they were prior to the 'marriage'. How ironic.

22

ALL STANDARD BEREAVEMENT POLICIES SHOULD DIE

As old as the dirt in which they should be buried, traditional Bereavement Leave policies still exist in some organizations. They typically stipulate the number of paid days an employee can receive to grieve for a loved one who passed. Adding insult to injury, some of these policies actually list the relatives that can be mourned with pay (e.g., mother, father, sibling, etc.)

The policy at our company is simple – take paid time off to grieve for anyone you cared for (including pets), for as long as you need. It's not radical at all. The policy works just fine and is truly appreciated by our employees.

If you feel that your organization could never implement such a policy because some employees will take advantage (e.g., the grandma who passes on twice), then you have the wrong employees working at your place.

23

SUCCESS IS BORING

If I was a mountain climber, I would never want to reach the summit of the mountain. For every step I took, I would want the summit to move up by length of that step. For me, there is so much truth to the phrase 'The journey is more important than the destination'. I would make one change to the phrase – 'The journey is more *fun* than the destination'.

Every time during my career, when I reached a new 'base camp' of success, I would find myself temporarily lost and wondering "What's Next?" I learned that getting there was the fun part and arriving at the destination did not bring me any intrinsic 'rush'. Sure there were promotions, a couple more bucks and eventually the corner office. Those only provided me about a minute of Dopamine. Nothing sustainable, so I would always look for another journey to take.

I found that those around me were way more impressed than I was with success. It did not take me long to recognize that societies' success definition was simply not mine. Plus, success is significantly harder to sustain than to achieve.

The challenges along the journey have been the greatest teaching moments, provided emotional highs and lows and opportunities to innovate, take risks and create. As I look back at my career, the highlight reel would include the peaks, valleys and wonderful people encountered along the way to the summit (which I thankfully never really reached). Attaining any level of success is not a memory, just another destination along the way.

I have met people that get stuck at a destination and are content to keep what they have, not take any more risks because they don't want to walk away from the success they finally attained. To me, that is not the summit – it's falling off the cliff of life.

24

SIMPLE IDEAS FOR A HAPPIER WORK LIFE

We tend to make our daily work lives much more complicated than they need to be. Keeping life simple is not an easy task, especially at work. But by focusing on the following ideas, you may find that you can condition yourself to manage everything at work and outside of work with a healthier perspective:

- Live in the present. You may have heard this idea before, but it works. Regretting something that you did yesterday and worrying about tomorrow is wasted energy. Yesterday is gone and tomorrow is not promised. The next hour is not even promised. Make the moments count as you can never have them back.

- Don't stay in a job that is not a fit. Regardless of whether it is your boss, the workplace or the work, it may be time to move on to the next opportunity. Try not to mentally quit and physically stay at a job that does not work for you.

- Take on one task at a time. Multi-tasking is a nice buzzword but can add immeasurably to stress and job dissatisfaction.

- Turn your phone off when you get home. Emails, texts, and other posts can wait until tomorrow. It may be tough at first but try it for a week. Unplugging is a great way to simplify your life.

- Every day attempt to make your focus to positively impact your family, co-workers, customers, and the community.

- Make today better than yesterday and repeat this approach tomorrow. Don't live for the weekend as living two out of every seven days is a horrible way to exist.

- Be home for dinner each night if you can (and don't forget to turn off the phone).

- Work hard at working smart.

- Hang out with people that make you better.

- Once you recognize there is no time to waste, you will make better decisions about how you spend your time.

- Don't hit the snooze button in the morning. Those extra minutes lying in bed add up. Think of the time you will be giving yourself to enjoy life if you just get up and get going!

- Ask yourself each morning – "How can I change the world today?" Then go out and do it.

- Exercise, sleep and eat healthy. The benefits of doing all three can be incredible.

- Allow yourself to laugh and have fun each day.

- Focus on the positive whenever possible.

- Be grateful. Be generous. Be humble.

- Find and then live your passion.

- Remember, you can re-boot your life any time you want.

You probably have some basic rules you live by. We make the life we lead, so why not make the very best day today that you can despite any hardship you may be facing. Every day is not promised to be a bowl of cherries. Quite the contrary. As we grow older, we realize that moments of happiness are fleeting. Seek to maximize those times and multiply those special moments.

When you look back and judge your life, hopefully you

can say that each day, you gave it your best regardless of the outcomes. When you do that, you will most likely have lived a life that had meaning, purpose and made a difference.

Don't ever underestimate your importance in this world. Towards the end of your career, you may realize that success was never about job title, money or status. These are all artificial and in the end, are meaningless. True life fulfillment and happiness result from being true to yourself and giving your time on Earth 100% effort. You'll see.

25

OVER THE RAINBOW

One of my favorite movies that teach leadership lessons is the *Wizard of Oz*. Virtually every character in the movie can be compared to a stereotypical leader or follower in today's workplace. From the Wizard to the Wicked Witch, the core characters demonstrate different approaches to leadership and how followers react to each leadership style.

For example, the Wicked Witch ruled based on fear and intimidation. And when she was finally done away with, via a bucket of water, all her past followers rejoiced with relief that the Wicked Witch was dead. Perhaps in your career, you have run into a few individuals who attempted to rule the organization in a similar fashion. Suffice it to say leaders like the Wicked Witch either don't survive the company or the company does not survive them.

The Wizard is another flawed character, portraying something he is not and getting away with it with followers unwilling to 'look behind the curtain' to see the real person at the controls. These individuals try to fake their way through their careers and if they ascend to a leadership position are eventually unmasked because they cannot deliver on their promises.

Of course, my four favorite characters are Dorothy, the Scarecrow, the Lion, and the Tin Man. Together they embody vital characteristics every leader should possess. Dorothy is the dreamer and visionary. The Scarecrow has the brains and the know-how to get the job done. The Lion represents courage. Vision, knowledge, and courage are critical for leaders. But they are nothing unless they possess what the Tin Man has – a heart.

26

DOGS RULE!

Dogs may be the almost-perfect species. If they could talk and perform the same tasks as humans, we would all be out of work. They have these incredible attributes that would play well in a work setting:

- Respect and treat people the same regardless of their race, color, religion, national origin, veteran status or sexual orientation. They don't need laws like Title VII of the Civil Rights Act to treat people without discrimination.

- Exhibit loyal – a key ingredient to sustaining the employee and employer relationship.

- Stay away from things that stink. The business lesson is to stay away from bad deals that seem too good to be true.

- Do not bark behind your back. If they have something to say, they let you know to your face and right away. How much better would workplaces be if we cut out the "hall talk" and rumor mill?

- Play nice and treat each other well.

- Provide unconditional love all the time. Employers that appreciate a diverse workforce thrive and improve the probability of attracting and retaining top people.

- Never take their family and neighborhood dog friends for granted. Likewise, people who consistently show up for work and put forth 100% effort should be appreciated.

- Love security, consistency, and predictability; so do humans, especially in their workplace.

- Rest well. The breaks they take are a good lesson on pacing our work, time off and family. Your career is a marathon that cannot be finished or won if you are in the *rat race.*

- The good dogs never bite anyone. Employees need to be respectful of each other as should employers be respectful of their staff.

- Work hard and retrieve sticks and *Frisbees* until

exhaustion. When you go to work, give it your all and make a positive difference in your organization.

- Are never shy about showing affection in public and are great listeners. If you are a manager, don't hesitate to recognize exceptional employee performance publicly.

- Will have a short but fulfilling life – guaranteed. In the big picture, our careers are also brief. We might as well make the days count and enjoy work while making a living. If you love your job, know your contributions, and believe in what you're doing you won't be living for the weekend.

We can learn much from our canine companions. Maybe they can't teach us how to build effective compensation systems, recruit better or increase profits, but they sure can provide lessons on how we should treat each other at work.

All the dogs we have owned at home over the years were enrolled and passed obedience class when they were puppies. What an experience! There is nothing quite like watching twenty strangers with new dogs pretending to have some control over their pets. If I weren't a part of the class, it would have been worth just pulling up a seat to watch. Interestingly, the dogs attending the class did not need the teaching; rather it was the dogs' owners who needed lessons. The dogs were, in fact the real teachers.

27

NOGOALZ

Many years ago, I was driving on the highway and spotted a license plate that read NOGOALZ. At first, I thought it was humorous, then realized that NOGOALZ pretty much summed up my career. My career success was due to taking one day at a time and giving 100% each day. Fortunately, the hard work paid off and I found myself consistently being in the right place at the right time.

I've never made a New Year's resolution or had formalized short or long-term goals. I did not want to be burdened by them. My daily focus has also been to prioritize family before anything else. I measured any success I enjoyed on how well I adhered to that prioritization and how well I performed as a dad, husband, and son, then an employee.

Though structured goal-setting is thought of as a critical key to achieving success, I do believe that everyone is unique relative to how they determine and achieve success in their lives. I am living proof that you do not need defined goals to be in alignment and achieve relative success. If goal setting helps you get there, more power to you as whatever works for you is a great formula.

28

SIZE DOES MATTER

"The bigger, the better" mantra plays well with many consumers and prospective employees as they often correlate size with success. Positive corporate brands are powerful and tend to provide 'halo effects' with anything associated with large growing organizations. But is the music always in sync with the dance?

Some folks love showcasing big corporate names on their resumes and in hopes that prospective employers will be in awe of the big company track record. And, that approach often works when the potential employer is another large organization. I have known a ton of people along the way who work or have worked for large companies. Few experienced a great workplace. They discovered they were just one of the thousands with little voice or impact on moving the company 'needle'.

Likewise, I have been fortunate to know many individuals in small and mid-size companies. Most love their jobs and their workplaces. They feel they have a say in the direction of their company, have a purpose in their role, and can make a positive impact.

There have been very few people I know that want their organizations to grow faster or get bigger. They know if that happens, they will end up with more work, same pay, increased stress, and job insecurity. If you are an organizational leader, ask your employees if they want their respective companies to grow fast. Their answers might surprise you.

Personally, I have worked for two mid-size organizations, one small company, and two worldwide billion-dollar operations. There is no comparison relative to my experience across the board. I learned that size does matter – the smaller, the better.

29

NO REGRETS

During your career, you will make hundreds of decisions. Some will be easy, and some will be incredibly challenging. And, as responsibilities and leadership roles expand, those decisions will make an impact on your personal life, career, company and of course others.

Looking back in time, you may find that some or many of your decisions might have been different if you knew then, what you know today. In fact, if you do not feel this way, you would be in a unique position.

We all make plenty of mistakes and that is how we all learn. It is repeating these mistakes when real failure comes into play.

Remember this – regrets cannot exist if you feel you are making the best decision at the time. No need to beat yourself up over 'spilled milk'. Channel your energy on the positive and recognize that your life is a journey. It won't be perfect, but if you trust your gut, most of the decisions you make will likely be good ones.

30

HOW TO MARKET YOUR COMPANY

_____

As organizations,we spend a lot of time and money to promote, brand, and market our respective businesses. Aside from all the vehicles used to channel branding and marketing messaging, customers, guests and vendors get an accurate picture of companies through the following:

How bills are paid– Some organizations still feel that it is good business to stretch out payments. Sure it may help cash flow, but it can hurt a company's reputation as being known as a slow payer on money owed for services rendered. Pay vendors on time when they accomplish the work promised. It's the right thing to do!

How your people answer the phone or greet guests– Seems like there is nothing that lasts longer than a first impression. Ensure that your employees are well versed in how to provide a great customer and guest experience every time.

Physical appearance inside and out – Whenever I visit a company I get to their location early and drive around their building and check out landscaping, cleanliness, parking lot, etc. When I enter and sign in, I typically ask the receptionist (when there is one) if I can use the restroom. My restroom "visit" is to check out cleanliness and sanitary conditions. I take the same approach when I am given a tour of their facility. The kitchen always tells a story of the culture as does office and cubicle set up, paint colors, lighting, and artwork.

The visuals on the outside and inside of the building provide me an initial impression relative to organizational pride and often correlates well with the level of employee engagement. This may not be a terribly scientific approach, but in most cases, it proves out to be accurate.

Website and social media – How others perceive your organization through your social media posts and website can have a dramatic impact on your reputation, sales and talent attraction. These 'electronic billboards' are often the 'front door' to your organization. A well-designed website that successfully tells your company's story can be incredibly effective to enhance your organization's image. Thoughtful and content-rich social media posts increase the probability that your organization's following will include prospective customers and job candidates.

Recruitment advertising – The classic print advertisement may be extinct. Corporate recruiters are recognizing that creativity in ads, whether they be online or print, are necessary to catch the attention of individuals actively seeking a new position or passive candidates. With the pool of top talent seemingly shrinking, the competition for these candidates has heated up and resulted in recruitment campaigns that are fun, interesting, eye-catching and innovative.

Do GREAT work – Your company's reputation for consistently providing high-quality services and products delivered on time and at the right price will often be your best marketing and promotional campaign.

How your company handles mistakes – Nobody's perfect and errors do occur despite the best efforts of your team. How issues are resolved with customers provides useful insight into a company's integrity and their commitment to backing their products and services.

Your employees – Every person you employ is a salesperson for your company. They are your representatives and ambassadors at work and outside of work. When you attract and retain high-caliber, top performing employees your company significantly increases the odds of ensuring that your workforce is making positive impressions with customers, guests and prospective employees.

What is communicated via your origination's promotions, branding, and marketing should align with reality. A marketing campaign should creatively present the real picture of your company, including culture, employees, products and services. When they do, they can be incredibly powerful and support the success of your business. Remember though, that real marketing occurs when "actions speak louder than words."

31

SOCIAL MEDIA IS NOT SOCIAL...IT'S JUST MEDIA

It's laughable to think that social media has brought us all closer together. There may be nothing that has eroded away our ability to truly connect as human beings at work and outside of work like technology and social media. They have forever changed how we communicate.

Technology certainly allows quick dissemination of content. Whether it is through mainstream media, co-workers, friends, or family, the content people share and how they share it shows up in many forms, pictures and videos. Regardless of how content transfers, there remains no substitute for in-person conversation.

Technology has allowed us to become lazy when it comes to trying to communicate the old-fashioned way. For instance we;

- have all probably seen people text the person who is in the same room with them or the individual who sends an email to the person in the office next door,

- yearn for real connections with each other but rely on texting for the tough conversations,

- stare at pictures and content while we are sitting down for dinner or relaxing with those we love,

- check in with our friends less than we check social media, and

- hold our phones in one hand while we hold the hand of someone we love.

Sadly, the substitution of verbal communication for the quick and easy text (or emoji) is routine, accepted and preferred by so many. Slowly, we are losing ourselves. The very essence of what separates us from machines is evaporating, and not too many people seem to care. It's a shame. Perhaps one day as people look back on their lives, they will realize all the moments they missed that were played out via keyboard. *#awasteoflife*

32

RIPPLES CAUSE WAVES

Let me start out be sharing with you my story of the 'magic pebbles':

Some pebbles at the bottom of a river bed never move. They are comfortable with calm, clear waters and not disturbing a thing. These pebbles simply exist. Some pebbles move along with the stream and go with the flow. They land wherever the 'river of life' takes them. Then there are the magical pebbles. They defy gravity and are able to swim and navigate their own paths down streams, rapids, waterfalls and eventually the great oceans.

These magic pebbles generate plenty of ripples in the water when they swim around. Magic pebbles are not liked by the idle pebbles laying calmly at the bottom of the river because the magic pebbles shake things up. Water gets turbulent and muddy. When this occurs, the river is just not the same anymore. The pebbles at the bottom of the river hope the magic pebbles go away soon so everything can settle down and get back to the 'way things always used to be'.

The magic pebbles love to make small waves and often are joined either by other magic pebbles or other pebbles interested in becoming magical. When groups of magic pebbles swim together, they bounce around and make small waves which eventually become big waves. Though these waves cause havoc for so many other pebbles, the waves are critical to the ecosystem of the river. Waves must be made to stir things up and allow the river to survive and thrive.

We all start out as plain ordinary pebbles, all dropped from the heavens into a calm stream or river. When dropped, we all make one ripple in the water at the beginning of our lives. Sadly for some pebbles, that is the only ripple they will ever make.

Perhaps we should measure our personal and professional success by the sum of the ripples and waves made at the end of our lives. You can change the world, but you need to start a ripple. One ripple and one day at a time. So when you get up tomorrow, ask yourself how you will change the world? Go out and make it happen. 'Get the finger' (Chapter 5), take a risk and make a difference. Repeat the next day and the next day and the next day.

Each day we can and often do change the world. What you do and say during the day alters our world, perhaps in even the tiniest bit, but it does change our world. You make history daily. Really.

We make slight ripples in our universe through our actions. Even if you are just accomplishing your to-do list, the world changes each time you perform actions that result in new outcomes.

What you say to people also causes ripple effects. For example, let's say today you help someone at work or share a kind word with them. The impact you make with them may be huge, and it was perhaps what you said or did that causes them to look at themselves in a more positive light. Their confidence and esteem get a boost, and they end up performing better at their job. Over time, their work gets noticed, and they receive a well-deserved promotion. This person goes on to earn more promotions and more money resulting in being able to support his or her children through college. One of his or her children goes on to become a medical researcher and discovers the cure for a deadly disease.

Guess what? All this may have started many years back because of what you said or what you did. You were the catalyst for a wave of change that altered someone's life and their future generations. Far-fetched example? I think not. It happens every day, everywhere on this planet.

You never really know the impact you can make on someone. What you should know is that your actions and words do count and make a difference.

As you drift off to sleep tonight, assess whether you made a positive impact with your family, friends, co-workers and in the community today. If you did, sweet dreams as you accomplished your purpose on earth today!

And that my friend is what a magic pebble does. Change the world, make history and you will eventually transform from a magic pebble to a rock star.

33

IMITATION IS NOT INNOVATION

Imitation often gets confused with innovation. Some organizations brag about their 'innovative' products or services when all they do is rip-off original ideas and make a few enhancements. This is not innovation – it is called improvement.

Innovators are the pioneers. They create something that is brand new. It take vision or perhaps just a crazy idea. Throw in a massive amount of risk-taking and you have yourself an Innovator. They change the world and inspire others to imagine new services and products that fill a market gap or even create a new market.

Imitators simply follow Innovators closely in their shadows and seek to capitalize on market opportunities. There is nothing wrong with that and in fact, consumers' benefit when Imitators copy Innovators. It would just be nice if the Imitators gave credit where credit is due.

34

WHO ARE YOU WORKING WITH?

———————

It is interesting how different some people are outside of work. Your co-workers may act one way at work and be a completely different person once they leave the work premises. Perhaps it is due to the workplace environment, expectations of professionalism or the 'guards' people put up to protect themselves on the job. Regardless of the reasons, it is a shame that authenticity sometimes lacks in the workplace.

This lack of authenticity can have a direct impact on the level of trust and working relationships among co-workers. For instance, it can be a challenge to work well with a co-worker when it is obvious they are putting on a facade. The more authentic a person is at work, the easier it is to get to know and respect them.

Even if some people attempt to hide who they truly are, true personalities often emerge in a variety of circumstances. If you want to understand a co-worker, observe their behavior in the following situations:

When they play competitive sports – If your company provides opportunities for co-workers to play in organized after-work sports leagues, how people play the games can give you great insight into their competitive nature and sense of fair play. A great example is the game of golf as it seems to bring out true character. How well people keep score, stick to the rules and follow golf etiquette provides great insight on an individual. Those who cheat on their scorecard, move their ball for a better lie, kick their ball into the fairway or from behind a tree, booze it up, get angry, disregard basic golf decorum and disrespect caddies/golf course employees may not be ideal co-workers or team players.

Social gatherings – How co-workers act at after-work functions and outings (e.g., holiday parties) are often excellent indicators if the person at work is the same person outside of work.

Under pressure – Does your co-worker go from *Dr. Jekyll* to *Mr. Hyde* when the pressure is on at work? How people handle the pressure of meeting deadlines, workload and change offers a glimpse into a co-worker's reliability when the 'heat' is on, and their ability to maintain composer in the most challenging of times.

Sense of humor – A good sense of (tasteful) humor goes a long way at work. The ability to smile, laugh, make light of tough situations and laugh at ourselves, create work atmospheres that are fun and enjoyable.

Participation in teams – How co-workers act in team situations showcase their ability to work well with others.

Complainers – Complaining is a lazy alternative to identifying solutions to problems then doing something to fix the issues. Complaining does nothing to advance organizational missions or a positive workplace atmosphere. Next time someone complains about anything to you, ask them what they plan to do constructively about the situation.

When something goes wrong– Mistakes happen all the time. How people accept responsibility for their mistakes reflects their ability to be accountable for their actions.

I do believe that you never really know whom you are working with if you only know them from the persona they portray at work. Ideally, we all find workplaces where we can be ourselves and not have to act one way at work and then be ourselves when we leave for the day.

35

MEETING EXPECTATIONS

Do you ever feel that you have so many meetings at work that you never get to what you want to accomplish during a workday? In-person office meetings do provide an important vehicle for communication with others. Whether they are one-on-one or with a group, how meetings are conducted often dictate their effectiveness.

If all or some of the meetings that you participate seem to be a waste of time, assess the following key components to an effective meeting:

Agenda – Perhaps you have participated in meetings where there was no set agenda, or the meeting organizer asked at the beginning of the meeting, "Now...why are we meeting?" Lack of agendas or direction allows the conversation to go in multiple directions. Meetings need focus to be effective.

Time – Isn't it interesting that most meetings are scheduled for one hour? Imagine what would happen if all your meetings where scheduled for 45 minutes or even 30 minutes. My guess is that the conversations would be more productive, focused and effective. Plus, you would gain a ton of time on your individual schedule. Try it at work for a week and I think you will be amazed how much you can accomplish in a shorter time frame. I'll also guess that no one will complain that office meeting time is reduced!

The time of day can also impact meeting effectiveness. Seek times that make sense for your business and your attendees. Also, be sensitive to what day of the week meetings are scheduled. For instance, meetings scheduled late Friday afternoons during the summer may not be as productive as a morning meeting scheduled earlier in the week.

Attendance – Having the right people attending your meetings starts with a good agenda. Understanding what needs to be discussed and accomplished typically dictates who should be in attendance. In addition, punctual attendance by attendees is important to stay on task and within the allotted time frame. Having key people consistently show up for meetings late can really throw off the momentum of a good meeting.

Expectations – Setting an expectation for attendees as to their level of participation can set the tone for a meeting. Active participation by all attendees really helps relative to understanding different perspectives. If attendees understand that meeting attendance often requires meeting participation, attendees are more likely to get prepared and understand the material to be discussed.

Meeting leadership – Every meeting needs a leader to ensure the agenda is followed, to facilitate the conversation, have ownership over the outcomes and identify next steps.

Logistics – Believe it or not, the location of the meeting can have a bearing on its effectiveness. Beyond the traditional conference room setting, consider non-traditional meeting places in and outside of your workplace. A change in scenery can do wonders for meetings that are traditionally housed in office conference rooms.

Shake it up – One of the criticisms of the traditional office meeting is that they lack variety. If you have a weekly sales meeting for example, consider a standing versus a sitting meeting. Assign seats so that people do not get too comfortable each week sitting with the same person. Utilize different ice-breakers to encourage conversation, smiles and laughter. There are dozens of ways to make your meetings different, and I dare say...fun! Imagine if attendees looked forward to your meetings, because they know that your meetings move along, stay on task and are a bit different each time you get together.

Fuel – Over my career, I attended hundreds of company and client meetings. I have seen a wide range of food and beverage offered – from a box of donuts to a seven-course meal (for lunch). When choosing food for guests, keep in mind the audience, time of day and try to keep it healthy!

Reduce Annoyances – This is one that could be a challenge for some people. Mandate that no one can ever present using PowerPoint slides that contain bullet points. Analogous to someone scraping their fingernails on a chalkboard, there may be nothing more annoying at a meeting than having bullet points read to you by a presenter. Also, request that everyone in attendance turn off their mobile devices and place them out of view. Last but not least, request that laptops be turned off and placed out of view. Meetings are for in-person conversation. Eliminating distractions will increase the probability that the dialogue is constructive.

In-person meetings are an every day reality of working in a business. They are essential to your operations and maintaining good communication within your organization. If they are run well they can be incredibly constructive and meaningful. Ironically, to get started in a new direction, have a meeting to discuss your modified approach for future meetings. Incorporate new and creative meeting office meeting strategies and you will find that you are meeting less often while getting more accomplished. Your toughest part after that is figuring out what you will do with all your extra time!

36

ALWAYS HAVE A CLEAR HEAD

————

I will never forget the reaction when I instituted a no-alcohol policy at our company when I first started as President of our organization. It was simple – do not drink while on company time including events where employees represented our organization. Though this program sounds like something out of Prohibition, it served us well. As a professional services firm, our people are our product. The impressions they make, whether a first or last impression, are critical to our success.

Each of our employees is an ambassador of our company

regardless of title. Plus, we received tons of positive public notoriety over the years, and with each passing year, the performance expectations of our company and our people grew. We never wanted to let a guest, client or employee down and as such wanted to ensure that each day we were putting our best foot forward. That is why we never wanted our employees to have even the slightest 'impaired' behavior.

Perhaps this view all started with a situation that occurred early in my career. I was employed by a firm that had an outstanding reputation in town for professionalism and exemplary work. We were all very proud of the reputation and worked hard each day to continue to earn our clients' trust.

Each year that firm hosted a client golf outing and dinner. One year, one of our associates drank (we did not have an alcohol policy at that firm) too much at the cocktail reception (and perhaps during the outing) and vomited on one of our best clients at the dinner. Our reputation soured that evening, and it could have been a complete disaster if it were not for an incredibly understanding and tolerant client (we did not lose the business). Nonetheless, after witnessing this episode I was convinced that alcohol, regardless of amount consumed, was going to put our organization at risk. More importantly, we had an obligation to do what we could to keep our employees safe and sustain a healthy work environment.

Do we hurt ourselves from a business standpoint with such a strict, no-alcohol consumption policy? Maybe. We know that some clients like to be 'wined-and-dined' to obtain their business. Since we do not play that game, perhaps we lose some dollars. But we do go to bed at night knowing that we do our best to support a great business model and the safety of our team and clients.

37

WORK DOES NOT MATTER THAT MUCH

———————

A long, long time ago human beings worked hard for their food, shelter, and family well-being. Life was simple. There were no policies, procedures, insurance, money, office politics, government bureaucracy, company bureaucracy, dress codes, paid time off, employee benefits, compensation, total reward programs, etc. In some ways, work and the workplace have become a complicated, tangled mess. Perhaps we have created a monster that we try to tame daily.

Why we have allowed work to become harder than it

should be is perplexing. That is why smart organizations have recognized that a key to sustained success is to keep things simple.

Work is full of artificial fluff that stands in the way of personal and organizational success. On your most challenging work days, remember that none of it matters compared to your family, friends, and good health. Keep these in great shape, and the work stuff becomes silly in comparison.

Remember, work and earning a living is important. Just not that important.

38

WHEN YOU KNOW IT'S TIME TO LEAVE

It is not unusual for organizations to conduct annual or semi-annual Engagement Surveys with their workforce. These surveys are intended to gauge the level of employees' satisfaction with their jobs, organizational leadership, and general work environment. The results of Engagement Surveys can be quite useful to management in identifying areas of needed improvement. When results of these surveys are communicated with employees and acted upon systematically and constructively, positive organizational changes can occur.

Engagement Surveys do not tell the whole story. There are always employees disconnected from their work, bosses, or organization. For whatever reason, the 'marriage' between the employee and their employer is failing. As with any marriage, both partners need to be interested in making the relationship work, or it is probably going to end up in a split. Organizational 'divorces' can be amicable, or they can be nasty. Neither is particularly fun and alters the life of the departing employee and culture of the organization they are leaving. Hopefully, the change is ultimately positive for both parties.

For organizations, there are some signs that surface that indicate an employee is disengaged with their job. These might include increased absenteeism, tardiness, missed assignments, lack of participation at meetings, increased defensiveness, argumentative, or general decreased job performance. Sometimes, employees who exhibit any of these, may not even realize they are 'showcasing' their dissatisfaction with their work, to their co-workers and manager. Though, deep down inside they wish they had a different job, boss, or place of employment. So, if some of the following describes how you're feeling, perhaps it is time to re-evaluate your commitment to your current job and workplace:

TGIF – you hate Mondays, have hope on Wednesdays ('hump day') and are thrilled when Friday arrives. You are living for two out of every seven days.

Unhappy – you feel consistently unhappy at work and can't wait for your workdays to end.

Complaining – you find yourself complaining quite frequently about work, to co-workers, and who you think are your confidants.

Happy when your boss is on vacation – when you are happy your boss is out of the office, this is a sign that things are not going well at work.

Apathetic – you find yourself caring less about the organization, your work or co-workers. Easy tasks become harder to accomplish, and you find yourself having to expend a great deal of energy just to perform basic work. Your heart is just not into your job. The excitement you may have once had for your organization and your work is gone.

Everyone else sees it but you – I believe that good character is doing the right thing when nobody's watching. What dictates whether people are genuinely engaged, and what is seldom covered in Engagement Surveys, is what you do when nobody is around to witness your performance.

Fully engaged employees are the ones who love what they are doing, know what they are doing, and believe in what they are doing. And, they do so without regard to witnesses or close supervision.

Remember that doing the right thing at work when nobody's watching is the difference between being a person of character or being considered a 'character' by your boss or co-workers.

Faking it – if you are disengaged with your job and workplace, there may be a tendency to go through the motions with the goal being to do just enough not to get fired. Unless you are an outstanding actor, faking your work will eventually be noticed.

I believe that most people want to be happy at work and outside of work. The research is clear that job satisfaction and job happiness are not necessarily aligned with money, good performance reviews, or promotions. These are important and reflections of a job well done, but sustained happiness on the job comes from within – you feel like you are at the right workplace, doing the right job, and are making a difference. You enjoy your co-workers, love the work environment, and believe in the company's purpose or mission. When that happens, you do not need your actions to be witnessed, to work hard and to do the right thing, because the person in the mirror knows you are fully engaged.

This is your life. You have options when it comes to working. You can find the right job and organization for you, where you can be happily 'married'. Conversely, if you accept anything less than a high level of job satisfaction and remain on the job, you basically end up quitting (on yourself) and staying in a bad situation. The choice seems obvious.

39

WHAT WE FORGET

As time moves on at work we tend to forget or take for granted events in careers that are so meaningful including:

Getting a job – if you have been fortunate to be employed for a while, perhaps you have forgotten what it means to get the call with a job offer, including your first 'real' job. Remember the nervousness and the elation of finding out that you were going to be employed and get a paycheck? In addition to money, work does wonders for one's self-esteem and confidence. It's important to remember what it was like because today someone is waiting for that call, someone is about to jump up and down with the news of a new job, and someone's life is

III

about to change with that call. This is a big deal and an exciting time that should be embraced and celebrated. Once we lose that appreciation, we have lost touch with the importance of work in our lives.

Getting a promotion – promotions are in most cases, the affirmation that a job was well done. People work hard to advance in their careers. They put in the hours, continue to learn and go above and beyond the expectations of the job. Promotions are earned and not given, and that is why it is worth making these a big deal!

Life events – what a joy it has been to witness our employees' life journeys. We have been fortunate to have a very low turnover of staff and have watched employees graduate from college, get married, get a house and have a family. Their kids grow and go off to college. Unfortunately, some employees' family or friends get ill and some pass. We watch the circle of life playing out in front of us from the sleepless nights with a newborn, to the sadness that engulfs those losing a loved one.

It is important that we take these times to reflect on how we felt during these events and provide support to our co-workers who are living it today. What we need to always remember is to never allow a procedure, process, money or day-to-day work activities dampen or minimize one of the most important attributes we all need to have at work: empathy.

40

SWEET FREEDOM

───────

I've never understood why people stay at jobs they hate or, in some situations, allow themselves to be disrespected by co-workers or their boss. Why don't they just leave the job if the situation cannot be corrected?

Perhaps it is easier said than done. There is nothing that provides individuals with more freedom to have job mobility than being a top performer. Be a superstar, and you can call your shots. Top performers have little to no tolerance for unsatisfying work, bad workplaces or poor bosses. They move on and move up because they have the confidence to do so.

Focus your energy on outperforming everyone at work,

in a job you believe in and one that you love. If you do that, you will find a lifetime of career options anytime and anywhere.

41

CREATING A GREAT WORKPLACE

There are some pretty easy ways to enhance your workplace. It is important to note that my suggestions are focused on attracting and retaining top performers. So if your organization is committed to the top performer talent management model, here are some ideas to help you develop a workplace people will love:

Expand your top performer population – Your business success is tied to the number of top performers you employ. They drive most of your success, so it makes sense to have as many on your team as possible. We want top talent for our local sports teams, so why not for our own workplace teams? Plus, top performers wanted to work with other talented top performers.

Paint colors – Consider using bright, energizing colors on your company's walls. That would include the interiors of factories, warehouses and distribution centers. Throw in some tasteful, fun and bright artwork and you have the beginnings of a workplace, that even on the gloomiest days shines bright.

Make some noise – Invest in some decent speakers throughout your building and pump in uplifting music. I've been to too many work settings where you can hear a pin drop. Unless your business mandates a quiet atmosphere, adding some pleasant music to the work setting does wonders.

Ask them – Don't forget to ask your top performers their ideas of how to improve your work environment. Their insight and thoughts may surprise you and they will appreciate being asked.

Productive work setting – Make sure your employees have the tools, technology and resources they need to get the job done.

Personalize – Let employees (tastefully) personalize their work-spaces.

What's on the walls – Consider hanging art and/or photographs on the walls that tell a story and have meaning. They are great conversation pieces and reflect the personality of your staff and workplace.

HVAC – When it comes to heating and cooling you probably can't please everyone at work. Yet, you can ensure that there is good airflow and temperatures are set at reasonable levels.

Great place to eat – There are the exceptional workplaces that remodeled their work spaces around kitchens and dining areas that reflect their company's culture. These 'hubs' provide centralized areas where employees can gather throughout the workday, collaborate, converse and socialize. They provide a way for all employees to get away from their work spaces to take a breather and enjoy a snack or meal versus one of the worst places to eat – their desks.

Keep them off balance – People love nice surprises and the workplace is no exception. I always feared routines as they often lead to 'ruts'. Ruts lead to monotony and monotony leads to boredom or frustration. To prevent staff from getting bored or in comfortable routines, I would surprise them at staff meetings, retreats and ordinary workdays throughout the year when they would least expect something to occur. From spot bonuses to bringing in an ice cream truck, there were countless ways we surprised staff, put a smile on their faces and continued to remind them that our workplace was different, fun and filled with tremendous people.

Can eat off the floor – A clean place to work is a basic assumption every employee should be able to make. Make no mistake, that workplace cleanliness sends a message to your staff and visitors that you care about your team and have organizational pride.

Dog and family friendly – Back in 1998 I brought my Labrador Retriever (Nikki) into the office to celebrate her birthday with our team. They could not believe we were going to allow dogs in the office. From that day forward, the pooches were welcome and have become a hallmark of our organizational culture. In addition, we let our team know that their children were welcome anytime. This took tremendous pressure off parents when there was a snow day, or some other situation came up when daycare or school attendance was a challenge. What productivity loss occurred by being dog and kid friendly was more than made up with the positive impact made on our team and their appreciation for a work setting that was nontraditional.

Sit or Stand – Having attractive and ergonomically friendly furniture is as important as any other resource or tool needed by your team to do their jobs. Whether it is a standing desk or a properly designed conference chair, furniture matters to people. Like brightly colored walls, carefully select fabrics and colors that are pleasing to the eye and complement your work setting.

What schedule? – The 9 to 5 in office job is changing and evolving. Thank goodness! Today, you can find dozens of variations of the traditional workday and workers, especially top performers, are appreciating the flexibility.

Show them the money – Employees expect companies

to pay very competitive wages and provide well-rounded benefits packages today. With a premium on finding and keeping good people, it is critical that companies assess their programs and ensure that they are meaningful and commensurate with job duties and responsibilities. And, don't forget to share the wealth through bonuses during financially successful years. Bonus programs are commonplace these days and a well-structured program recognizes both team and individual performance.

Keep people safe – Many years ago, workplace safety was often just thought of as an issue for manufacturing due to the nature of the work. Today, workplace safety goes well beyond the use of equipment and includes preventing hostile work environments, harassment and workplace violence. People want to go to work at a safe place. It is incumbent upon organizational leaders to invest energy and dollars into programs that increase the probability that employees can feel and be safe in a place where they can enjoy their work and make a positive difference.

Thank you – Workplace recognition programs are vital to a healthy corporate culture. Team and individual performance should be recognized through cash and non-cash programs. Whether it is simply saying thank you or providing tangible awards, employees want and need to know they are appreciated and contributing to the success of the business.

Giving back – Today, employees expect their organizations to make a positive difference in the community. It may be a community project, donation or allowing your team paid time off to volunteer. Whatever form it takes, community service is fast becoming an important 'pillar' in the foundation of a great place to work.

Care – Organizational leaders need to care more about their people than profits.

None of the ideas outlined above are hard to accomplish. It is a matter of commitment to building a great workplace. The pieces and parts are not complicated. They just need a relentless approach and continuous process improvement to make it happen. When I lead ERC, our management team would spend at least 50% of the week focused on our employees and figuring out new and better ways to build a great workplace. We believed that if we were successful with a developing an enhancing an exceptional place to work, we would attract the best and success would follow.

Fortunately, we were right.

42

THE LAST LEADERSHIP ACT

In 2017 I initiated a leadership transition at our company. Business was great, our financials incredibly strong, and we continued to be on a roll. After nearly 20 years of leading our business, I felt it was time personally and professionally to initiate a leadership transition.

Over my career, I had seen too many leadership transitions flop for all kinds of reasons. Perhaps it was poor execution, egos or lack of succession planning. Regardless of the reason, a poorly executed transition of power typically leads to disaster, layoffs, unnecessary stress placed on employees, or corporate in-fighting.

Usually, there are two winners in these scenarios; the exiting CEO and the lawyers.

In the best-case scenario, the transition is smooth, understood internally and externally and welcomed with excitement by staff, customers and the organization's Board. The organization moves forward better and stronger.

I believe that a leader should transition power effectively and exit with great timing and grace. It is the last act of leadership at any organization by any CEO. What a leader accomplishes leading up to his/her final departure is only two-thirds of their job. The last third is the leadership transition and it needs to be well-executed.

Remember that no one recalls your first day on the job, but they will remember your last.

43

MISCELLANEOUS THOUGHTS

Here are a bunch of random thoughts that did not seem to fit anywhere in particular in the book. Perhaps one or two of these will resonate with you:

- Time does not heal all wounds.

- Share and discuss financial statements with your employees each month.

- Be prepared for a new employee's first day on the job.

- Everyone at work can be a leader.

- Employ at least one intern a year.

- Respect is the foundation of a great workplace for top performers.
- Most people hate performance reviews.
- Lawyers are great when they are on your side.
- You can tell a lot about a company by the cleanliness of their restrooms and kitchens.
- "We always have done it this way" is a sad excuse for not trying something new.
- "You can't do that" is excellent motivation for innovators.
- "Thank you" costs nothing and should be given out freely.
- Always accept a resignation.
- Return everyone's phone calls within 24 hours.
- Hand-written notes of appreciation stand out, especially in this era of social media.
- There are plenty of people who are sick, scared, stressed or in a tough life situation who would love your 'bad day' at work – it is nothing compared to what they are facing. Be grateful for the opportunity to have today.
- Always ask a consultant how they know their recommendations really work. Ask them if they ever implemented their recommendation as a practitioner

versus a consultant. Remember that great ideas are ones that actually work.

- There are no history books about people doing average things.

- The best way to give back to the community is to raise great kids

- Everyone at work deserves equal respect, regardless of pay, tenure or title.

- Discover your 'Why Not?'. Figure out what is holding you back from living a full life and decide whether you want to break through the barrier.

- One day will be your last day at work. Treat today like that day.

44

WHAT I WILL MISS MOST

———

Oh, the great people I have met along the way,
they were the reason to get up each day.
It was never the work, the title or dough,
just the opportunity to be with people I know.
Stay long enough, and they become a part of you,
bonded together forever through work like glue.
Memories made that touch the soul,
as we strove to reach our company goal.
I will not remember details of the grind,
just thoughts of those people stuck in my mind.
What laughs we had, and moments shared,
no wonder people retiring are scared.

———

Spent my life working to change the status quo,
rebelling against dumb stuff that we all know.
I think we made a difference at all my places of work,
even at jobs where the boss was a jerk.
Grateful understates how I feel,
to have a career filled with zeal.
It was a ball, a hoot and a game,
yet it does end and what a shame.
I may forget the things that got done,
but for sure will not forget the fun.
What I will miss are the great moments in time,
as to forget them would be a crime.
What a wonderful ride it has been,
I leave it bittersweet with a tear and a grin.

45

WHAT'S NEXT?

—————

I announced my 'retirement' from ERC effective December 31, 2018. As this book goes to print, I still am about 4 months away from completing an incredible run at the company. It has been a great experience and I am grateful for the opportunity. I leave the organization better than how I found it and believe our team made a massive, positive impact on the business community. We changed many business leaders' thought patterns and people's lives. We made a difference.

Ironically, we forged our job security through taking risks and creating workplace practices that we had never seen implemented in other organizations. We hired talented and creative individuals who stuck around, found ways to outperform competitors and managed to prioritize their family over their jobs. Pretty cool!

So now what? I have no idea. Much of the retirement 'advice' I researched suggests that in addition to having a financial plan, that a retiree should have a personal game plan. This plan would include expanding a social network, finding part-time work and enjoying hobbies. That is all well and good, but I have never planned much in my life (see the NOGOALZ chapter). The fun for me has always been and will continue to be not knowing what is 'around the corner'.

Here is what I do know. I will continue to seek ways to make a difference each and every day with my family and in the community. In addition, I will continue to pursue my passion for changing workplaces for the better and helping people dislodge their fears of taking action personally and professionally to do the same.

Unfortunately, our lives are a one-shot deal. I hope I get to live a lot longer and continue to make an impact, appreciate life and enjoy my precious family. I love to write and really hope you enjoyed this book. It's just a guess, but I bet there is another book swirling in my head, yet to be written. Stay tuned. In the meantime, my wish for you is simple...

May you find peace, alignment and happiness in your life.

88542536R00080

Made in the USA
Middletown, DE
10 September 2018